PERSONA

FOOTBALL

KEN SHELLITO

CARNIVAL

William Collins Sons & Co Ltd
London . Glasgow . Sydney . Auckland
Toronto . Johannesburg

First published by William Collins 1988
© Mander Gooch Callow 1988

ISBN 0-00-194705-2

Printed in Great Britain
by Warners (Midlands) plc

Designed and produced by
MANDER GOOCH CALLOW
Illustrations: Roger Wade-Walker
Front Cover Photograph:
Tony Stone Photo Library London

Contents

Introduction

In these pages you will find 25 fun games with over 40 full colour illustrations, specially designed to show you exactly how to make the most of your soccer abilities and improve any weaknesses in your game. You will learn all you need to know, from choosing and looking after your kit to beating opponents with accurate passing and dazzling ball control, as well as painless heading and dribbling of which many first division players would be proud. You don't need any special equipment and you can play many of the games by yourself or with friends. Using the laws in brief you can even organize your own matches.

How do you know you are improving? Well, there are charts and record pages for you to mark and record your very own personal best in each group of skills, so you can see your progress. You can keep a record of the progress of your school or favourite league side too.

You can improve your soccer skills and have fun at the same time and more importantly achieve your very own personal best.

THE LAWS IN BRIEF

The Field of play

This is the field of play. You may play on a smaller pitch, but it should be no smaller than 75 metres by 55 metres.

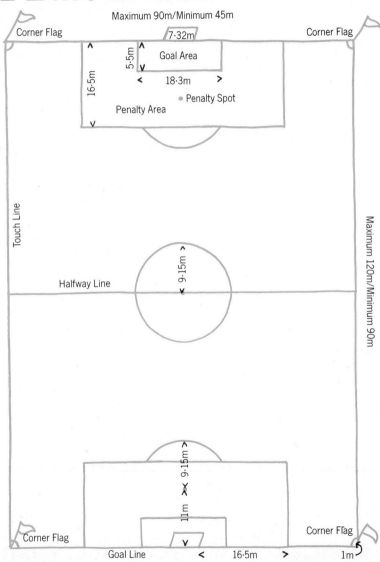

The full, official rules of the game are available from the Football Association, but these are the main points.

The ball
In an official game, the ball should measure between 68-71 cm, round and weigh 396-453 grammes when the game starts. For young players we suggest a smaller ball (see equipment). You are not allowed to change the ball unless the referee says that you may.

The teams
You must have 2 teams, with 11 players on each side, one of whom must be the goalkeeper. In a competition where substitutes are allowed you may use them in a match. Any of the players may change places with the goalkeeper if you tell the referee first.

The kit
Players must not wear anything that might hurt another player. Bars and studs on boots must match those in the safety standards.

The referee
The referee is there to make sure the game is played to the rules. His decision about any point of fact in the game is final, as far as the result is concerned.

The linesmen
You should have 2 linesmen who help the referee to control the game and keep the rules.

The length of the game
An official game is 45 minutes each way, unless both sides agree to a shorter or longer time. Schoolboy's matches are usually 35-40 minutes each way.

Starting the game
You choose ends by tossing a coin. The winner of the toss chooses either the ends or to kick off. The referee blows his whistle and the ball is kicked off from the centre spot into the opposing team's half. Every player must be in his own half and every player in the opposing team must be 9.15 m. away from the ball. The player taking the place kick is not allowed to play the ball again, until it has been played by another player. After a goal is scored, play is started in the same way by the team against whom the goal is scored. At half-time the teams change ends, and the team which did not start the play, kicks off.

Ball in and out of play
The ball is out of play when it has wholly crossed the goal-line or touch line, or if the ref. stops the game.

Scoring
Normally, a goal is scored when the whole of the ball has crossed the goal-line, between the goal posts and under the cross-bar, unless it is scored illegally (with hand or arm).

Off-side
If a player is nearer the goal-line of the opposing side, than is the ball at the moment when the ball is played he is off-side. Unless:
1. He is in his own half.
2. There are two players of the other team nearer the goal-line than he is.
3. An opponent last touched or played the ball.
4. He received the ball direct from a goal-kick, corner, throw-in, or when it was dropped by the ref.

Fouls and Misconduct

If a player does any of the following things, he must have a free-kick given against him, or a penalty if the offence took place in the penalty area:

1. If he kicks or tries to kick an opponent.
2. Trips an opponent.
3. Jumps at an opponent.
4. Charges an opponent dangerously.
5. Charges an opponent from behind, unless the opponent is obstructing the player.
6. Strikes or tries to strike an opponent.
7. Holds an opponent.
8. Pushes an opponent.
9. Handles the ball.

An indirect free kick, from which a goal cannot be scored will be given against a player who does any of the following:

1. Plays in a dangerous way.
2. Charges when the ball is out of play distance.
3. Obstructs an opponent on purpose.
4. Charges the goalkeeper when he is holding the ball.
5. When playing goalkeeper, takes more than 4 steps whilst holding, bouncing or throwing the ball in the air and catching it again, without letting it go so that it can be played by another player or when he wastes time on purpose.

Free-Kick

Free-kicks can be either direct, from which a goal can be scored or indirect, from which a goal cannot be scored. Opposing players must stand 9.15 m. or more away from the ball, when the free-kick is taken. A player cannot score directly against his own side from any free-kick.

Penalty-Kick

A penalty-kick must be taken from the penalty mark. All the other players except the opposing goalkeeper must stand outside the penalty area until after the kick has been taken. Like a free-kick the player who takes the penalty is not allowed to play the ball again until another player has touched or played it.

Throw-in

When the ball has gone wholly over the touch-line, it must be returned to play. The throw-in is not taken by a player from the side that touched it last. It is taken by a player from the opposite team. The thrower must use both hands and throw the ball over and from behind his head. Part of each of his feet should be on or behind the line at the moment he throws the ball. A goal cannot be scored directly from a throw-in.

Goal-kick

When the ball has passed wholly over the goal-line it must be kicked directly back into play from a place inside the half of the goal area, nearest to the point at which it crossed the line. The ball must be kicked beyond the penalty area before it's in play.

Corner-kick

A corner-kick is taken when the whole of the ball passes over the goal-line, outside the part between the goal posts. When it was last played by a member of the defending side, the ball is returned to play by a member of the attacking side. It is played from a corner of the field. The corner flag must not be moved but a goal can be scored from this kick.

FOOTBALL EQUIPMENT

BOOTS

Your boots are the most important piece of equipment that you will buy, so you must get the right boots for you and then you must look after them.

Pick the style of boot that you like best but choose the size very carefully. Football boots will always stretch. When you try on your new boots do not wear socks. Make sure that they fit your bare feet snugly. Boots which fit when you are wearing socks will be too big.

When you have bought your boots, you must take care of them. Before you wear them have a look at them and if you have chosen screw-in studs, unscrew them carefully. Ask your mum or dad for a tin or jar of Vaseline. The studs screw into the boots by a thread. Dip this thread into the Vaseline. Before you screw them in again, walk about in the boots to help loosen them up. This will stretch them a little for when you play. Screw the studs in for your first game.

After you have played your game, clean your boots straight away. Take the laces out and brush as much of the mud off as you can. Rinse them well with water. Hang them upside down to dry slowly. Never put them near a fire or radiator to dry quickly, or they will become hard and shrink. When they are dry, polish them carefully with good wax shoe polish. Don't put the laces in until just before you wear them again. At least once a month, unscrew the studs and dip the threads in Vaseline again. This will stop your studs from rusting into the soles. It is most important that you never play in boots which are too big. Your foot will slip about inside your boot and your ball control and touch will not be as good.

YOUR FOOTBALL

When you choose your football you must have the right size. Players under eleven, unless they are tall for their age, should play with a size four. Smaller players should try a size three. Playing with the right size ball will be a great help to ball control.

Taking care of the ball is as important as taking care of your boots. Always wash the ball after use and make sure that the stitches are really free of dirt, otherwise they will rot. Do not pump the ball up too hard. If you can feel a very slight dent in the ball when you push with your thumbs it will be about right.

PADS

Always wear shin pads when you play football.

KICKING THE BALL

Kicking the ball does not mean that you must try to kick it out of sight every time. The aim is to kick with just the right force, in the right direction.

You can do this if you put your non-kicking foot alongside the ball.

Kick the ball with your full instep (the top part of your foot just under your boot laces.)

As you kick, follow through with your kicking foot. Lean forward so that your body and knee are over the ball. If you are aiming for a target that is some distance away, you must use more force to reach it. If the target is near you must use less force. The only way to find out how much force to use for different distances is with lots of practice. Try these games with friends. (We have called our players John, Jim, Peter, Paul and Tony.)

FORCE AND DIRECTION
for 2 players

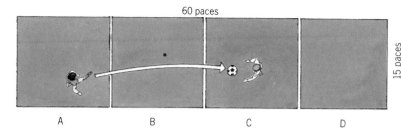

60 paces

15 paces

A B C D

Measure, and mark out boxes as shown. You can use chalk, sticky white tape, or anything which will mark out the areas.

John stands in box A and kicks the ball to Jim who is standing in box C. John must use just enough force to get the ball to Jim's feet without letting it drop into box B. Jim then stops the ball (without using his hands) and from inside his box, kicks it back to John, once again clearing box B. By trial and error, John and Jim will find out just how hard to kick the ball to clear the box and reach the other player's feet easily.

TIP Do not kick the ball too hard. When John and Jim can kick the ball to each other easily. Jim moves into box D and the ball must clear both B and C. When this also becomes easy, Jim steps outside the box and the ball must clear B, C and D. Finally, both players move outside the boxes and the ball must clear all four boxes easily. You can mark your success rate on the chart as you improve.

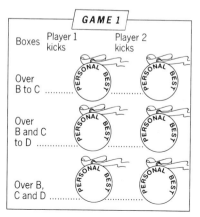

GAME 1

Boxes	Player 1 kicks	Player 2 kicks
Over B to C	PERSONAL BEST	PERSONAL BEST ....
Over B and C to D	PERSONAL BEST	PERSONAL BEST ....
Over B, C and D	PERSONAL BEST	PERSONAL BEST ....

GAME 2

TARGET PRACTICE
for 1 or more players

For this game we move to the pitch to use skill as well as force and direction. The aim is to hit the crossbar with the ball. Place the ball on the six yard line and aim for the crossbar. Score how many kicks it takes for you to hit the crossbar 4 times. Move the ball to the penalty spot and aim for the crossbar again.

How many kicks does it take to hit the bar 4 times from here? Move to the penalty line area and do the same as before. Finally aim for four hits from the penalty area arc line. Mark your scores on the chart. If you are playing with a friend and the net is down, play either side of the net.

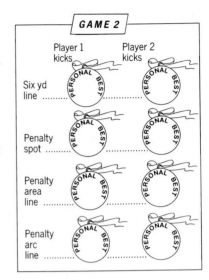

GAME 2

Player 1 kicks   Player 2 kicks

Six yd line .... PERSONAL BEST   PERSONAL BEST

Penalty spot .... PERSONAL BEST   PERSONAL BEST

Penalty area line .... PERSONAL BEST   PERSONAL BEST

Penalty arc line .... PERSONAL BEST   PERSONAL BEST

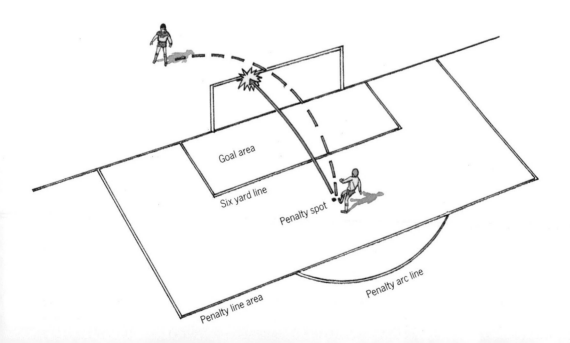

Goal area

Six yard line

Penalty spot

Penalty line area

Penalty arc line

BETWEEN THE POSTS
for 2 players

John and Jim stand either side of the rope and each takes 15 paces away from it. John must kick the ball hard and low, between the posts and under the rope, to Jim. He does this by remembering to put his non-kicking foot alongside the ball. He keeps his head down and leans forward, with his body and knee over the ball. He kicks with his full instep and follows through with his kicking foot. Jim stops the ball (again without using his hands)

and plays it back to John in exactly the same way. Neither John nor Jim plays the ball back first time. They each concentrate, set the ball up and without rushing, kick the ball when they are ready. They play the ball like this until every step comes easily to them.

Score how many times out of ten you can kick the ball to one another without going either high or wide.

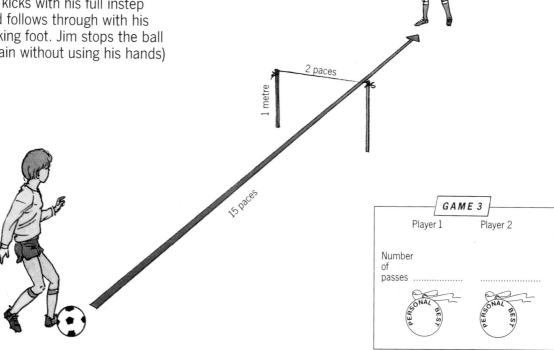

2 paces

1 metre

15 paces

GAME 3

Player 1   Player 2

Number
of
passes ....

PERSONAL BEST   PERSONAL BEST

11

HEADING

The ball is in the air for a great deal of the time during a game of football. So heading the ball is an excellent skill. Goals can be scored from a header, which always looks impressive. Heading the ball can also be used to set up shooting and is used in good defensive play. It is very important to head the ball correctly and to make sure of this when you practise. This is because not only will you lose control of the ball if you head it badly, but also because it can sometimes hurt. The first thing to remember is ALWAYS to play the ball on your forehead. If you do and you keep your eyes open, you will see the ball on to your forehead and after heading, you see it all the way to the target. Secondly, stand with one foot in front of the other and rock backwards and forwards to keep your balance. Thirdly, let your arms hang comfortably at your sides, that will help with your balance. Finally, remember to keep your mouth either open or closed for the whole of the header, if you close it half way through, you could bite your tongue.

GAME 1

HEAD-TO-HEAD
for 2 players

Peter and Jim stand face-to-face and head the ball to one another. They try to head it ten times before they lose the ball. They do not head the ball too hard.

GAME 2

HEAD-TO-TOE
for 2 players

Jim throws the ball to Peter, who heads the ball back to Jim's feet for Jim to control. Jim picks the ball up and throws it to Peter to head again. They do this ten times. Then Peter throws the ball and Jim heads it for 10 counts.

TIP When you are heading the ball down to a player's feet, do not let your neck go loose, keep it stiff and direct the ball downwards, bending forward.

Score how many times you both head the ball without losing control of it.

GAME 1	
Player 1	Player 2
Headers	....
PERSONAL BEST	PERSONAL BEST

GAME 2	
Player 1	Player 2
Headers	....
PERSONAL BEST	PERSONAL BEST

In games 1 and 2 the players should be at least 5 metres apart.

GAME 3

LONG AND SHORT
for 3 players

Tony stands in the middle and throws the ball to John, who heads it back to Tony. Tony heads it back to John, who heads it to Paul. Paul heads it to Tony. Tony heads it to Paul. Paul heads it to John who heads it to Tony. They try to continue like this for two complete circuits. They are practising both short and long headers.

Score how many circuits you manage before you reach your target.

5 metres   5 metres

GAME 4

HEADER BALL
for 2 players

To play this game you will need a badminton net. Paul and Peter stand either side of the net. They will head the ball over the net to each other aiming to get height into their headers. This is good defensive heading and good practise for jumping headers, where timing is important.

Score how many headers you can do in a sequence. Your target is 6 headers.

TWISTS AND TURNS
for 3 players

Tony, Jim and John stand in a triangle. Tony serves the ball to John, who heads the ball to Jim. They try to direct their headers at an angle of 45 degrees. To re-direct the ball, John twists his body. His feet stay firmly on the ground. He turns his body, to play the ball on his forehead he does not flick the ball or strike it with the side of his head. Jim then serves the ball to John, who heads the ball back to Tony and so on.

GAME 1   Circuits ....   PERSONAL BEST

GAME 2   Headers ....   PERSONAL BEST

GAME 3   Restarts ....   PERSONAL BEST

HIGH SKILL PRACTICE

for 14 advanced players

Mark out, or find a pitch with goals, 30 metres apart. The pitch is 20 metres wide. The players divide into two teams and play normal handball. The difference is that they can only score by heading the ball into the goals. They can make as many passes as they like. The player cannot run with the ball, he must pass the ball as quickly as he can. Try to hand pass at interesting angles to find openings to score with a good header.

Score how many times you restart before you can make 20 headers in a row and change the sequence.

BALL CONTROL

You will have noticed that in the kicking games you are told to stop the ball without using your hands. This is really ball control. If you can get the ball under control and set yourself up for the kick quickly and skilfully, you will have the advantage over your opponent in a game. Juggling the ball is a very good practice to improve your ball control skill. You can do a great deal to improve your skill by yourself as the first games show.

 GAME 1

JUGGLING ON THE FOOT
for 1 player

Stand in the square and pick up the ball, dropping it on to your foot. Do not lift your foot too high. Keep the ball below shoulder height and let it drop low. This helps you to keep your balance. The aim is to keep the ball on your foot for ten touches in a row. If the ball touches the ground you must start again.

GAME 1	
Number of touches	
Ten touches Date	PERSONAL BEST

For these games, mark a square 5 x 5 paces.

GAME 2

JUGGLING ON THE THIGH
for 1 player

Stand in the square and drop the ball on to your thigh. Once again, aim to juggle the ball on your thigh, without letting it touch the ground, for ten touches. You must keep your thigh at the right level (waist high) and lean your head back slightly, or the ball will hit you in the face. If you bring your thigh up too high, the ball will go over your shoulder. If you do not bring your thigh up high enough, the ball will fall forward onto the ground.

JUGGLING ON THE HEAD
for 1 player

Stand in the square with one foot in front of the other to help your balance. Bend your knees and use them like springs, to help you get your forehead underneath the ball and keep it in the air. You will have to lean back to head the ball and this will stop you from

falling backwards. You must head the ball with your forehead and NOT with the top of your head. Keep your eyes open, so that you can see the ball coming and move your head so that it lands on your forehead. Keep your tongue away from your teeth. Once again aim for ten touches.

When you can score ten touches with each part of your body, you are ready to combine these skills in a high skill practice.

HIGH SKILL PRACTICE

GAME 4

JUGGLING WITH THE BODY
for 1 player

Still in your square drop the ball on to your right foot. On the third touch, play the ball a little higher and catch it on your right thigh for two touches. On the third touch play the ball a little higher and play it onto your forehead for two touches. On the third touch pass it to your left thigh for two touches. On the third touch, play the ball to your left foot for the final three touches. This completes the circuit of your body.

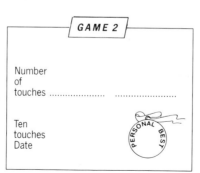

GAME 2

Number
of
touches ....

Ten
touches
Date

PERSONAL BEST

GAME 3

Number
of
touches ....

Ten
touches
Date

PERSONAL BEST

GAME 4

Date
completed
circuit ....

Number
of
circuits ....

Personal
Best
date ....

BOX BOUNCES
for 2 players

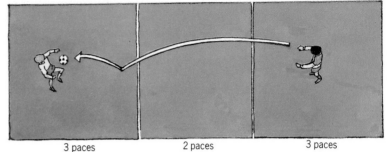

3 paces

3 paces   2 paces   3 paces

Measure and mark out a grid as above.

John stands on the far line of box A and throws the ball so that it clears box B, bounces only ONCE in box C to reach Jim in box C. Jim must control the ball, keeping it off the ground with either his foot, thigh or head. He can have no fewer than 3 touches and no more than 8. Jim then passes the ball back to John, clearing box B. It must bounce only ONCE in box A, before John controls it, keeping it off the ground with either his foot, thigh or head. John too is allowed no fewer than 3 touches and no more than 8 before passing back to Jim in

the same way. When John and Jim can control the ball easily in this way they can also control the ball on their chests, and then kick, control and return the ball without letting it bounce on the ground at all.

Score how many times you can pass the ball backwards and forwards in this way before the sequence is broken. Remember that you are helping each other so your service and return must be good.

GAME 5	
Number of passes in sequence	....
....	....
....	....
Personal Best date	PERSONAL BEST

AGAINST THE WALL
for 1 player

Find a stretch of wall at least 10 paces long and mark out a playing area (see diagram).

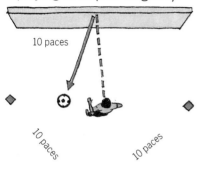

10 paces

10 paces

10 paces

Stand in the middle of the playing area between the markers. Play the ball against the wall. When it comes back to you, control it and dribble it around any one of the markers to your starting position. Don't rush, concentrate on controlling the ball.

HIGH SKILL PRACTICE

As you get better, start by throwing the ball against the wall so that it comes back to you in the air, as a real test of your control.

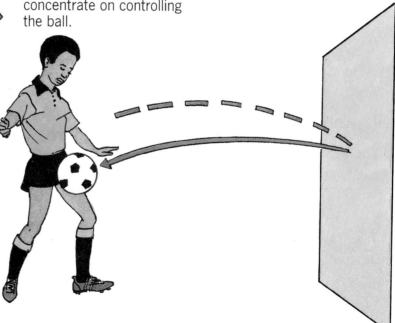

GAME 7

TOUCH PRACTICE
for 5 or more players

All the players stand around in a circle. The aim is to keep the ball in the air and in the circle. Each player must play the ball TWICE. The second touch must be a pass. You can move into the circle to keep the ball in the air, the circle is just a guide. Remember this is a touch practice so do not play the ball hard.

DRIBBLING

The first thing to remember about dribbling with the ball is that you should be perfectly balanced. This is most important, so that you can change direction at any given moment. It will be a great help if you remember these tips.

Keep the ball close to you at all times to stay in control of it. Say to yourself 'I must keep touching the ball.' Don't run too fast. Always remember when you are practising that it is more important to do things slowly and get them right. Don't rush and get tired, that is not practising.

GAME 1 WHISTLE STOP
for 2 players

John dribbles the ball around keeping it close to him. Jim blows a whistle whenever he chooses. John must stop, with his right foot on the ball and his left foot alongside or close to the ball to keep good balance. John starts dribbling again and on the next whistle, stops with his left foot on the ball. Once again keeping his balance. He starts dribbling again but at the next whistle, he stops the ball with his right knee only, he does not touch the ball with any other part of his body. At the next whistle, he stops the ball with his left

knee and then with both knees. When John can do each of these exercises 5 times in a row, he will stop the ball at the whistle by sitting on it. To do this he must have the ball close to him at all times. John and Jim then change places and Jim dribbles and John has the whistle. When you can do these well, try a real test of skill.

John has the ball and Jim has the whistle. John dribbles the ball and at the whistle, stops the ball with the sole of his foot. He pulls the ball back and at the same time turns his body. John is right-footed, so he pulls back with his right foot and pulls his right shoulder back, so that he is facing the other direction. When he has turned fully, he stops the ball with his right knee, so completing a full turn, under full control. Jim then takes a turn with the ball and John blows the whistle.

GAME 2

BALL SLALOM
for 1 player

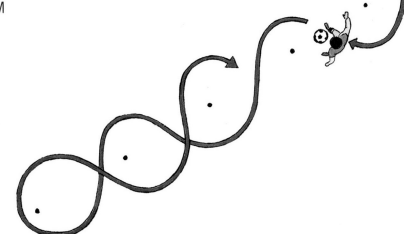

Place a line of markers one pace apart. Dribble the ball in and out of the markers, through the gaps. Do not race through, take as much time as you need to get to the end of the line without touching the markers. Work on keeping your balance throughout and use any part of your foot. When you can do this easily, move through the line using just the inside of your foot. When this becomes easy, dribble up and down the line, using only the outside of your foot. This will help you to move your body across the line of the ball. Finally, go up and down the line using just one foot, this will bring in all the skills you have been practising. Just remember take your time, keep the ball close to you, so that you can always touch it and move the ball in any direction.

GAME 3

WRONG FOOTING
for 2 players

Place two markers 4 paces apart. Peter and Paul stand in the middle of the space between the markers, with the ball between them. Paul has the ball and must dribble to either marker A or marker B and reach it before Peter. On a count of three they both move. Paul aims to fool Peter into thinking that he is aiming for marker A (for example) when he is going for marker B. The ball must not cross the line and neither must Peter and Paul. Paul must turn his upper body to fool Peter into starting out on the wrong foot (see illustration). Paul must use all the skills he has practised for dribbling, both feet, both the insides and outsides, perfect balance and complete concentration and ball control if he is going to win. When he has reached the marker they return to the middle, Peter has the ball and tries to wrong-foot Paul.

Score how many times you reach the marker before your friend.

Player 1   Player 2

....
Name   Name

Score ....   Score ....

PERSONAL BEST   *PERSONAL BEST*

....
Name   Name

Score ....   Score ....

PERSONAL BEST   *PERSONAL BEST*

....
Name   Name

Score ....   Score ....

GAME 4

ROUND AND ROUND AND IN AND OUT
for 1 player

Place a line of markers as game 2. This time your aim is to dribble in and out of the gaps between the markers, up and down the line. Before moving to the next marker you must dribble all round the one before. Try using the inside of your foot on all markers and then the outside of your foot.

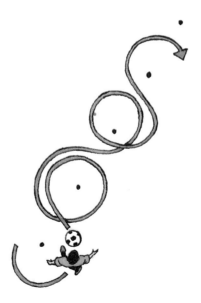

PASSING THE BALL

The passing of the ball is a vital part of any player's ability. To kick the ball to another player in a pass you must use a different part of your foot.

For short passes
Make sure that your non-kicking foot is alongside the ball and keep your head down and your body and knee over the ball. Use the inside of your foot to kick the ball and follow through with your kicking foot.

For long passes
Make sure that your non-kicking foot is alongside the ball and keep your head down and your body and knee over the ball. Bring your kicking foot back as far as you can without stretching and let it swing forward naturally. Your instep will strike the ball and remember to follow through with your kicking foot.

GAME 1

ONE-TO-ONE
for 2 players

Put down 2 markers 3 paces apart. John stands one side of the markers and Jim the other. John passes the ball to Jim, without kicking too hard, between the markers. He keeps the ball close to the ground. Jim controls the ball and passes it back to John. When this is easy for them, they move the markers so that they are 2 paces apart and continue the sequence.

Score how many passes you can make without hitting the markers or passing wide.

Score how many times you pass without going wide or hitting the markers.

GAME 1

Number of correct passes ....

....

....

Personal Best date .... PERSONAL BEST

GAME 2

TWO-TO-TWO
for 4 players

Put down your markers as game 1. John and Paul play to Jim and Peter. John passes the ball between the markers to Jim. Jim controls the ball for Peter and Peter passes the ball back, between the markers to John, who controls it for Paul. Paul passes it to Peter, who controls it for Jim and Jim passes it back to Paul who controls it for John. This way everyone takes a turn at control and at passing.

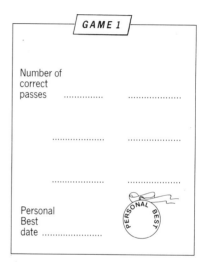

TIP Do not make it too hard, you are helping each other.

GAME 3

CORNER PASSES
for 3 players

Mark a square 10 metres by 10 metres. Each player starts in a corner. The player opposite the empty corner has the ball. To encourage good passing angles, no player may pass or move across the square. They must only pass or move along the sides. If you practise this exercise you will find that there is an amazing improvement in your passes. John stands in corner A, Peter in corner B and Jim in corner D, corner C is empty. John has the ball. John may pass along the sides to either Jim or Peter. If he passes to Peter, Jim must move to empty corner C, so that the corner opposite Peter (D) is empty. Peter may then pass, either to Jim or back to John. If he passes to John, Jim must move back to the empty corner (D). If Peter passes to Jim, John must move to empty corner (D) to be ready for a possible pass from Jim.

When John, Jim, and Peter feel happy that they have improved their passing, Paul joins in to play defender. The others pass the ball to their left or right down the sides of the square. It is Paul's aim to get between the players to take the ball. John, Jim and Peter can still only move along the sides. Paul can move in any direction. If the boys have got their passing angles right, Paul can only stop one passing movement, so they must pass to the free player, move and start again.

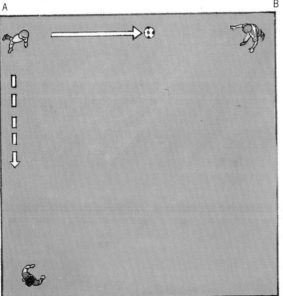

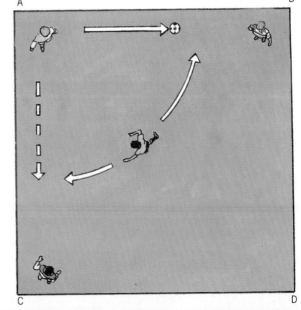

GAME 4

PIG-IN-THE-MIDDLE
for 3 players

Pace out and mark three squares. The aim is to improve short, accurate passing.

B

C

A

10 paces

10 paces

before Jim gets the ball. Jim can only get the ball if Peter or Paul give it to him. If Peter does give Jim the ball, he must then take a turn as 'pig'. If it is Paul who loses the ball then he must take his turn in the middle.

Score how many passes you make before changing 'pig'.

Paul stands in square A and Peter in square C. Jim is in square B. Paul and Peter must pass the ball (below waist height) to each other. Jim must try to intercept their passes. Paul and Peter can have as many touches as they like, and must move about in their squares to make good angles for one another's passes. Jim can move anywhere in his square to try to intercept. Peter and Paul are trying to get six passes in

GAME 4

'Pig' Player 1

....

Name

Score ....

PERSONAL BEST

'Pig' Player 2

....

Name

Score ....

PERSONAL BEST

'Pig' Player 3

....

Name

Score ....

PERSONAL BEST

PASS AND SHOOT
for 5 players

Mark a goal area if you can't find one to play in. Place 3 markers (see diagram).

Paul is in goal, Peter is at marker A, John at marker B, and Jim at marker C. Tony is the only passer. Tony passes to Jim. Jim sets up the ball for Tony to continue his run. When Tony reaches the ball, he passes to John. John sets up the ball while Tony continues his run. When Tony reaches the ball, he passes to Peter. Peter sets up the ball for Tony's shot at goal. After the shot Tony goes to marker A, Peter to B, John to C and Jim becomes the passer. They play on in this way until everyone has had a turn and the set-ups and passes are accurate.

Score the number of accurate set-ups, passes and goals scored.

Passing and shooting at goal are brought together in the next game. For both, you need to control the ball and be accurate. Remember not to move too quickly, set up your moves carefully. Both your passes and your shots must be accurate. Remember you are practising passing not shooting. The shot at goal is a reward for good passes and set-ups. If either is not good, you must start again.

ROUND THE CLOCK
for about 12 players

The players form a circle 15 metres from the player in the middle. He must pass the ball to each player in turn, going clockwise round the circle. As the player receives the ball he must control it, before passing back to the player in the middle. He must not play the ball first time. When every player has received and passed the ball, the player at 12 o'clock changes places with the one in the middle and they play round the circle again.

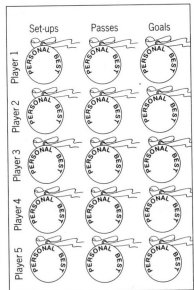

VERSUS _____

DATE _____

HOME _____ AWAY _____

1. _____ 1. _____
2. _____ 2. _____
3. _____ 3. _____
4. _____ 4. _____
5. _____ 5. _____
6. _____ 6. _____
7. _____ 7. _____
8. _____ 8. _____
9. _____ 9. _____
10. _____ 10. _____
11. _____ 11. _____

SUBS _____ SUBS _____

_____ _____
_____ _____
_____ _____

NOTES/GOAL SCORERS _____

_____
_____
_____
_____

VERSUS _____

DATE _____

HOME _____ AWAY _____

1. _____ 1. _____
2. _____ 2. _____
3. _____ 3. _____
4. _____ 4. _____
5. _____ 5. _____
6. _____ 6. _____
7. _____ 7. _____
8. _____ 8. _____
9. _____ 9. _____
10. _____ 10. _____
11. _____ 11. _____

SUBS _____ SUBS _____

_____ _____
_____ _____
_____ _____

NOTES/GOAL SCORERS _____

_____
_____
_____
_____

VERSUS _____

DATE _____

HOME _____ AWAY _____

1. _____ 1. _____
2. _____ 2. _____
3. _____ 3. _____
4. _____ 4. _____
5. _____ 5. _____
6. _____ 6. _____
7. _____ 7. _____
8. _____ 8. _____
9. _____ 9. _____
10. _____ 10. _____
11. _____ 11. _____

SUBS _____ SUBS _____

_____ _____
_____ _____
_____ _____

NOTES/GOAL SCORERS _____

_____
_____
_____

VERSUS _____

DATE _____

HOME _____ AWAY _____

1. _____ 1. _____
2. _____ 2. _____
3. _____ 3. _____
4. _____ 4. _____
5. _____ 5. _____
6. _____ 6. _____
7. _____ 7. _____
8. _____ 8. _____
9. _____ 9. _____
10. _____ 10. _____
11. _____ 11. _____

SUBS _____ SUBS _____

_____ _____
_____ _____
_____ _____

NOTES/GOAL SCORERS _____

_____
_____
_____